FIGURAL PLANTERS

A Pictorial Guide

With Values

Kathleen Deel

77 Lower Valley Road, Atglen, PA 19310

This book is dedicated to the memory of my brother, Russell Mayo, who died of cancer in 1993. How he would have loved to see this book in print!

CIP Data:

Library of Congress Cataloging-in-Publication Data

Deel, Kathleen.
   Figural planters: a pictorial guide with values / Kathleen Deel.
      p. cm.
   ISBN 0-88740-970-9
   1. Figural planters--Collectors and collecting--Catalogs.
   2. Figural planters--History--20th century--Catalogs. I. Title.
NK4695.F54D43   1996
738.3'8--dc20   95-26286
                    CIP

Printed in Hong Kong
ISBN: 0-88740-970-9

Published by Schiffer Publishing Ltd.
77 Lower Valley Road
Atglen, PA 19310
Please write for a free catalog.
This book may be purchased from the publisher.
Please include $2.95 for shipping.
Try your bookstore first.

We are interested in hearing from authors
with book ideas on related subjects.

Contents

Acknowledgements

My heartfelt thanks go to my enter-the-door, quick-look-around, ready-to-go, long-suffering husband, Elmer, who had to learn the art of patience; to number one daughter in Massachusetts, Debbie Mitchell, who trudged with me through mud, bone-chilling cold, 100 degree heat, and pouring rain at Brimfield to ferret out hidden treasure; to number two daughter, Kim Lambert, who served her apprenticeship as a child in the flea markets of New England and now scours the highways and byways of North Carolina in search of elusive vases to add to my collection; to my friend, Jean Payne, who loaded her van with so many lovely planters on a trip to Pennsylvania that she had to mail her clothes back home; to my friend in Philadelphia, Ruth Worthington, who graciously contributed many beautiful vases to enrich this book; and to my employer, The United Company, whose financial support, in the guise of a bi-weekly paycheck, made all this possible.

Introduction

Several years ago I became a collector of lady head vases. While searching for these vases, I began to notice other planters which I found equally appealing. These vases were primarily used by florists in much the same manner as the head vases, and were imported, principally from Japan, by the same familiar companies: Napco, Relpo, Rubens, Inarco, and others. I particularly looked for the beautiful Christmas and Valentine planters with their bright colors and marvelous workmanship. Soon the Raggedy Ann and Andy planters caught my eye, followed by the baby planters and the lovely ladies in their fancy dresses. As time went on, I began purchasing prime examples of every type of imported floral planter I could find, and the idea for a price guide began to take shape.

Figure 1

At the present time these figural planters are readily available at antique shops, malls, and flea markets. While the majority of the vases are still reasonably priced, I have seen an escalation in price of the holiday planters and the better examples of some of the other figural vases. If one is fortunate, it is possible to find a few at yard sales at bargain prices. A trip to a local flower shop may unearth a treasure or two, but, more importantly, it will give you an opportunity to observe the type of planter currently being used in the floral industry. The newer ceramic planters are often imported from Taiwan, and even Sri Lanka and Haiti, but, for the most part, they lack the exquisite detail of the older planters. A prime example of the old and the new is shown in Figure #1. Notice the clear detail of the older planter on the left, in stark contrast to the planter on the right on which the detail has been reduced to a blob, for want of a better word. On your foray into the world of hearts and flowers, also take note of the type of floral container which is in popular use at the present time. Just about any type of container, made out of any type of material, is now being used, and many times the flower arrangement is enhanced by the addition of balloons or stuffed animals.

Figure 2

Figure 3

It must have been a challenge for florists to come up with a credible flower arrangement using plastic flowers which are not nearly as pliable as the silk flowers now in common usage. I always consider it a plus when I find a planter with the older plastic flowers still intact. Many times the baby planters will still contain their pretty pink and blue arrangement, as in the happy elephant on wheels in Figure #2. The most elaborate arrangement I have ever encountered is the one in the large white Madonna shown in Figure #3. White flowers in a white vase with a touch of green, a truly beautiful display! However, more often than not, the flower arrangement will be missing and the only hint that it ever existed will be a trace of florist's clay in the bottom of the vase. Sometimes a planter will be found which is marked and stained from having held a live plant but many of the planters can be found in pristine condition, never having been used at all.

Some of the planters shown in this book are actually part of a series, and trying to track down a complete set can be a frustrating task. The little girls pictured in Figure #4 are part of a group which probably contained a total of seven, one for each day of the week. It would be a real challenge to find them all, but what a delightful addition to a collection they would make! The Christmas planters shown in Figure #5 are also part of a series. Their outfits are basically the same with slight variations, and are numbered in sequence. Shown in Figure #6 are two planters, alike except for the size variation, numbered 456L and 456S. Head vase collectors are already familiar with this numbering system, for variation in size and style is standard for those vases as well, showing the close parallel between the two types of planters.

Figure 4

Figure 5

Figure 6

The pricing in this book reflects the range of prices I have encountered in many trips to antique shops and flea markets in the eastern part of the country. From time to time I have seen exorbitant price tags attached to some of the holiday planters, and this price fluctuation is not reflected in this price guide. I have used the price range at which these planters will most often be found, and at which I would be willing to purchase a planter for my own collection. Planters with cracks, missing paint, or broken appendages are not in perfect condition and are worth much less than the price shown, regardless of what the seller would like you to believe. I do, on occasion, purchase a planter in less than perfect condition, but only if it is one which I believe to be rare and which has a defect which is not too noticeable. Any item bought with resale in mind should be purchased in mint condition only. If the item is bought for one's own collection, the heart can sometimes overrule the head. For instance, if I were to find a Raggedy Ann or Andy or an especially beautiful holiday vase that I did not have and had not seen before, I would probably purchase it with the thought in mind of replacing it with a better one at a later date.

Buy the planters that you, yourself, particularly care for and your collection will bring you happiness. It is not the quantity of vases that you amass, but the quality of the ones you choose that will make your collection outstanding. May you have as much joy in the collecting as I have had!

Animals

Although green puppies, lions wearing yellow shoes, and white cats carrying lavender umbrellas are not a normal everyday occurrence, they add to the charm of these fun-loving vases. There are plenty of conventional animal planters for those who prefer more realistic images for their collections.

Left: **1** Neidco Japan, 4.75" **$10-$12.**
Right: **2** Napco K2222, 4.5" **$8-$10**

Left: **3** Napcoware C7087, 6" **$12-$15**
Center: **4** Inarco, 5.5" **$12-$15**
Right: **5** Ucagco China Co, Japan, 6" **$12-$15**

Left: **6** 7767, 6.25" **$10-$12**
Center: **7** Relpo 6901, 6" **$10-$12**
Right: **8** Relpo KH1023, 5.75" **$10-$12**

Left: **9** Brinns, Japan, 6" **$10-$12**
Center: **10** Napco C-9002, 5" **$10-$12**
Right: **11** Napco, 6" **$10-$12**

Left: **12** No Mark, 5.25" **$12-$15**
Center: **13** 1961, Napco M53375, Bedford, Ohio, 4.25" **$12-$15**
Right: **14** E-4006, 5.5" **$12-$15**

Left: **15** Lefton H6974, 6" **$12-$15**
Center: **16** Napcoware 7201, 4" **$12-$15**
Right: **17** Napcoware 7087, 7" **$12-$15**

18 Japan, 6.25" **$12-$15**

19 C-2533, 6.5" **$12-$15**

Left: **20** 1964, Samson Import Co 97C5497G, 6" **$18-$20**
Right: **21** Relpo 6409, 6.5" **$10-$12**

22 Japan, Wall Pocket, 5.25" **$18-$20**

Left: **23** Napcoware 7439, 5.5" **$10-$12**
Center: **24** Ardco C-3323, Japan, 4.5" **$10-$12**
Right: **25** 1971, Rubens Originals, S.LA. 5121, 6" **$10-$12**

26 Enesco E-6207, Gold Finch, 4.5" **$12-$15**

27 Nancy Pew 4282, Japan, 3" **$12-$15**

15

Left: **28** Napco K4153, 4.5" **$10-$12**
Right: **29** Enesco, 5" **$10-$12**

Left: **30** Japan, 4" **$10-$12**
Center: **31** No Mark, 3.5" **$10-$12**
Right: **32** Japan, 4" **$10-$12**

Left: **33** Rubens, 6" **$10-$12**
Center: **34** Rubens Japan 3453, 4.5" **$10-$12**
Right: **35** K2688, 6" **$12-$15**

Left: **36** Lefton H4906, 5.5" **$12-$15**
Center: **37** Japan, 6" **$12-$15**
Right: **38** No Mark, 5.75" **$12-$15**

Left: **39** Inarco E-3259, 5.5" **$10-$12**
Center: **40** Inarco, 4.5" **$10-$12**
Right: **41** Nancy Pew 4271, Japan, 5.5" **$10-$12**

Left: **42** C2767, 6" **$12-$15**
Right: **43** Lefton H5766, 6.25" **$12-$15**

Left: **44** Lipper & Mann 16/653, 4.5" **$12-$15**
Right: **45** Sonsco Japan, 5.25" **$12-$15**

Left: **46** Inarco E-1636, 5.75" **$12-$15**
Right: **47** Napcoware 6917, 5.75" **$12-$15**

Left: **48** Relpo 6090, 5.5" **$10-$12**
Right: **49** Napcoware 251, 6" **$10-$12**

50 Rubens, 6.5" **$10-$12**

51 R/B Japan 1326, 5.25" **$12-$15**

Left: **52** No Mark, Wall Pocket, 4" **$12-$15**
Right: **53** No Mark, 4" **$12-$15**

55 No Mark, Wall Pocket, 5" **$12-$15**

54 No Mark, 5.5" **$12-$15**

56 Napcoware C-5425, Pheasant, 5.5" **$12-$15**

Babies

The ingenuity of the baby planter designers is amazing. Take one baby, add a pink and blue color scheme, and let a fertile imagination do the rest. The most plentiful of all the types of planters, baby vases run the gamut from rather humdrum bootees and utilitarian potties, to musical elephants with drums and train engines with smiling faces. A collection could be limited to just one type of baby planter, such as lambs, or could embrace a wide selection, whichever one preferred.

57 Napcoware, 4.5" **$15-$18**

58 Relpo A-1597, 5.5" **$15-$18**

Left: **59** Ardco Japan, 5" **$10-$12**
Center: **60** 1959, Samson Import Co, Relpo 405B, 5.5" **$12-$15**
Right: **61** Rubens 593BB, 5.5" **$10-$12**

Left: **62** 8571, 4.5" **$12-$15**
Center: **63** E-2952, 6" **$15-$18**
Right: **64** 1323, 4.25" **$10-$12**

Left: **65** Napco 4.5" **$10-$12**
Right: **66** 1409, 5.5" **$15-$18**

Left: **67** Inarco E-2445, 5.5" **$12-$15**
Right: **68** 1963, Inarco E-1583, 5" **$15-$18**

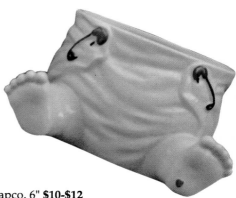

Left: **69** Napco, 6" **$10-$12**
Right: **70** 1977, Enesco E-9213, 3.5" **$10-$12**

Left: **71** Relpo 6358, 6.5" **$15-$18**
Right: **72** Brinns Japan, 6" **$12-$15**

Left: **73** 1961, Samson Import Co, Relpo 431B, 7" **$15-$18**
Right: **74** 1961, Samson Import Co, Relpo 431A, 7" **$15-$18**

Left: **75** No Mark, 5.5" **$15-$18**
Center: **76** Napco 7789, 5" **$10-$12**
Right: **77** 1263, 4.5" **$12-$15**

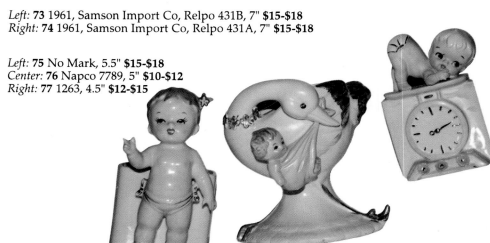

Left: **78** Napco G2181, 5.75" **$10-$12**
Right: **79** S288A, 5" **$8-$10**

Left: **80** Inarco CB-2070, Musical, 5.5" **$12-$15**
Right: **81** Inarco CB-2070, Musical, 4.5" **$12-$15**

82 Rubens 595, 5" **$15-$18**

Left: **83** Relpo 6831, 6" **$12-$15**
Right: **84** Napcoware 9957, 7" **$12-$15**

Left: **85** Napco C-5575, 4.5" **$10-$12**
Center: **86** 1960, Samson Import Co 5112B, 5.5" **$15-$18**
Right: **87** Rubens 637, 3.75" **$8-$10**

Left: **88** Relpo KH7094, 6.25" **$12-$15**
Right: **89** Japan, 7" **$12-$15**

Left: **90** 1957, Relpo KH761, 3.75" **$12-$15**
Right: **91** Relpo 6235, 2 pc set, 5" **$15-$18**

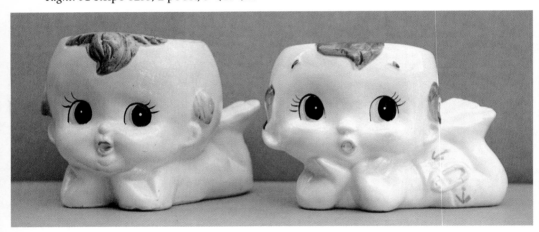

Left: **92** Rubens, 4.5" **$8-$10**
Right: **93** Rubens 3450, 4.25" **$10-$12**

Left: **94** Rubens 301, 3.5" **$8-$10**
Center: **95** No Mark, 3.25" **$6-$8**
Right: **96** Napcoware 7047, 3.25" **$8-$10**

Left: **97** Japan, 3.5" **$6-$8**
Center: **98** Japan 7951, 5" **$8-$10**
Right: **99** Relpo, 3.5" **$6-$8**

100 Dickson, 3.5" **$12-$15**

Left: **101** Japan, 3.25" **$6-$8**
Center: **102** Lefton 4642, 7" **$18-$20**
Right: **103** C-6906, 3.5" **$6-$8**

Left: **104** Napco C-5387, 3.25" **$8-$10**
Center: **105** 1965, Samson Import Co, Relpo 5643, 5.5" **$18-$20**
Right: **106** Rubens 299B, 4.25" **$8-$10**

Left: **107** C-2544, 5.75" **$10-$12**
Right: **108** Inarco E-3169, 4" **$10-$12**

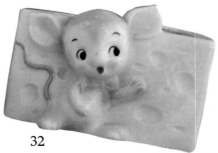

32

Left: **112** Lefton 5711, 6.25" **$12-$15**
Right: **113** Napcoware C-8580, 6" **$12-$15**

Left: **109** No Mark, 4" **$6-$8**
Center: **110** No Mark, 3.5", **$6-$8**
Right: **111** Relpo 6113, 3.75" **$6-$8**

Left: **115** Napcoware 1817, Musical, Brahm's Lullaby, 4.25" **$12-$15**
Center: **116** Parma by AAI A-8580, 4.25" **$10-$12**
Right: **117** Parma by AAI A-833, 4.75" **$12-$15**

114 C-7053, 5.5" **$18-$20**

Left: **118** Napco C6909, 4.75" **$8-$10**
Right: **119** Parma A-617/A, 4.5" **$8-$10**

Left: **120** Rubens 662M, 4.25" **$12-$15**
Center: **121** 1395, 4.25" **$12-$15**
Right: **122** Relpo A1471, 4" **$12-$15**

Left: **123** No Mark, 5" **$10-$12**
Center: **124** Napcoware C-7709, 5" **$12-$15**
Right: **125** Rubens 3299, Japan, 4" **$10-$12**

Left: **126** Nancy Pew 7944, Japan, 4.25" **$10-$12**
Center: **127** No Mark, 3.5" **$10-$12**
Right: **128** Lego 8218, Japan, 4.25" **$10-$12**

Left: **129** Japan, 5" **$12-$15**
Center: **130** Napcoware 3095, 4" **$8-$10**
Right: **131** Napco 2424, Musical, Brahm's Lullaby, 4.5" **$12-$15**

132 C-6700, 3.5" **$10-$12**

Left: **133** 1959, Rubens Originals 511, 5" **$15-$18**
Right: **134** Shafford Original 4176, Wall Pocket, 3.5" **$15-$18**

Left: **135** 1961, Samson Import Co, Relpo 4315, 5.5" **$12-$15**
Center: **136** 1956, Relpo 512B, 7.25" **$15-$18**
Right: **137** Rubens 325B, Japan, 5.75" **$10-$12**

Left: **138** 1961, Samson Import Co, Relpo 5129B, 4.5" **$12-$15**
Center: **139** 7272, 6" **$18-$20**
Right: **140** Rubens 572, 5" **$12-$15**

Left: **141** No Mark, 5.75" **$10-$12**
Center: **142** Ardco C-2399, Japan, 6.5" **$18-$20**
Right: **143** Ardco, 6" **$10-$12**

Left: **144** Rubens 679, 3.25" **$12-$15**
Right: **145** Rubens 1045M, Japan, 6" **$12-$15**

Left: **146** Inarco E-3676, 5" **$15-$18**
Right: **147** Napcoware 8573, 6.25" **$18-$20**

Left: **148** C-1522, 4" **$8-$10**
Center: **149** Rubens 690M, 5.75" **$15-$18**
Right: **150** Inarco E-4939, 4.25" **$8-$10**

Left: **151** Napcoware C-8849, 5.5" **$12-$15**
Right: **152** 7792, 6" **$15-$18**

Left: **153** Japan 4922, 5" **$12-$15**
Right: **154** 4953, 4.75" **$15-$18**

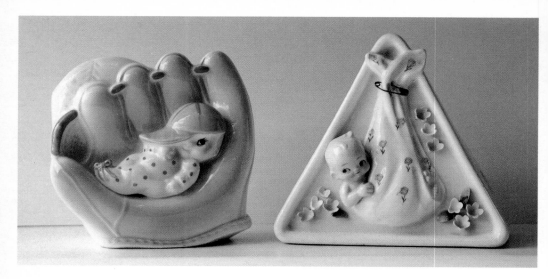

Left: **155** Rubens 577, 5" **$12-$15**
Right: **156** 4606, 5.25" **$10-$12**

Left: **157** Ardco Japan, 5" **$8-$10**
Center: **158** Rubens 3433, 4.5" **$10-$12**
Right: **159** KKC C-2654, Japan, 4" **$8-$10**

Left: **160** Relpo 6675, 4" **$10-$12**
Center: **161** 8692, 5" **$12-$15**
Right: **162** Napco C-3503, 3.5" **$8-$10**

Left: **163** lK1842, 4.75" **$8-$10**
Center: **164** Rubens 612, 6" **$12-$15**
Right: **165** No Mark, 4.5", **$8-$10**

166 Napcoware C-8019, 5" **$18-$20**

Left: **167** Relpo 6040, 3.5" **$8-$10**
Center: **168** Napcoware 8594, 5.5" **$12-$15**
Right: **169** Napcoware 222, 4" **$8-$10**

Left: **170** Rubens 3291, 6" **$15-$18**
Right: **171** 1962, Samson Import Co, Relpo 5361A, 4.5" **$12-$15**

Left: **172** Ardco C-2656, Japan, 3.25" **$8-$10**
Right: **173** Napcoware C-7056, 4.75" **$12-$15**

Left: **174** 282, 4" **$10-$12**
Right: **175** Inarco E-5083, 4.25" **$8-$10**

Left: **176** No Mark, 6.5" **$12-$15**
Right: **177** Napcoware C-2284, 3.75" **$8-$10**

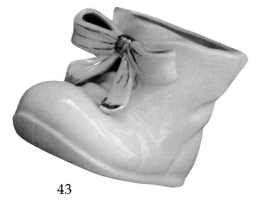

43

Left: **178** 1984, Lefton 04133, Japan, 3.75" **$10-$12**
Right: **179** Lefton 03855, Japan, 4" **$10-$12**

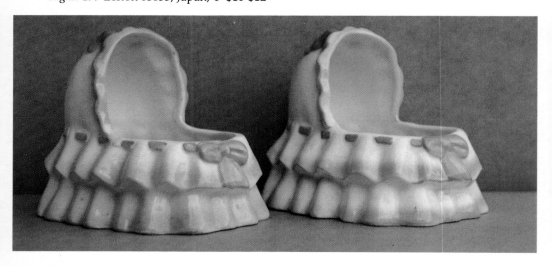

Left: **180** Napco, 5.5" **$8-$10**
Right: **181** Napco, 5.5" **$8-$10**

Left: **182** No Mark, 4" **$10-$12**
Right: **183** Lefton 3638, 3.25" **$12-$15**

184 Ardco C-4201, 4" **$10-$12**

Left: **185** Nancy Pew 7705, Japan, 4" **$8-$10**
Right: **186** Relpo 6015, 4" **$10-$12**

Left: **187** 565L, 3.25" **$6-$8**
Center: **188** My-Neil C66049, 3.5" **$6-$8**
Right: **189** Rubens 1052SX, 3" **$6-$8**

190 Napcoware C-8056, 6.5"
$15-$18

Left: **191** Napcoware, 4.25" **$8-$10**
Center: **192** Nancy Pew Giftwares, Japan, 5" **$10-$12**
Right: **193** No Mark, 5.25" **$8-$10**

194 377, 3.5" **$10-$12**

195 Napcoware C-8312, 7" **$15-$18**

Left: **196** Inarco E-4311, 6" **$12-$15**
Right: **197** C-8054, 5" **$12-$15**

Left: **199** Napco 900, Musical, Rock-a-Bye Baby, 7" **$12-$15**
Right: **200** Napcoware 1817, Musical, Rock-a-Bye Baby, 4.5" **$12-$15**

198 Rubens 3278, Musical, 5.25" **$10-$12**

Children

It is difficult to pass up a planter depicting winsome children, especially one which is well designed. Little boys are shown playing baseball and football, fishing, and doing chores. Whether make-believe firemen or rootin', tootin' cowboys, they are always active. Little girls are shown with dolls and puppies, bedecked in beautiful dresses and fancy bonnets. They like to get dressed up and wear their pretty outfits to the ice cream parlor. Teenagers haven't changed much over the years; they still like music, sports, and talking on the telephone.

Left: **201** Sanmyro Japan, 6.25" **$18-$20**
Right: **202** Sanmyro Japan, 6.25" **$18-$20**

Left: **203** No Mark, 5.5" **$15-$18**
Right: **204** No Mark, 5.5" **$15-$18**

Left: **205** Napcoware C-8225, 7.5" **$12-$15**
Right: **206** Napcoware C-3709, 6.5" **$12-$15**

Left: **207** Inarco E-4063, 6.25" **$15-$18**
Right: **208** E-4157, 5.5" **$15-$18**

Left: **209** Inarco E-3210, 5.25" **$12-$15**
Center: **210** No Mark, 7" **$12-$15**
Right: **211** Japan, 5.75" **$12-$15**

Left: **212** Rubens 467, 4" **$15-$18**
Right: **213** Rubens X399, 4" **$15-$18**

Left: **214** Caffco E-3090, 6" **$15-$18**
Right: **215** Japan A-21, 6.5" **$15-$18**

Left: **216** No Mark, 5.5" **$12-$15**
Right: **217** No Mark, 4.25" **$12-$15**

Left: **218** No Mark, 6" **$15-$18**
Center: **219** Relpo A-1754, 5.5" **$15-$18**
Right: **220** 1959, Napco C-45288, 6" **$15-$18**

Left: **221** Rubens 5153, 5.5" **$10-$12**
Right: **222** Rubens 5156, 6" **$10-$12**

Left: **223** No Mark, 5.5" **$12-$15**
Right: **224** Ucagco Ceramic Co, 5.25" **$12-$15**

Left: **225** Japan, 4.5" **$12-$15**
Center: **226** No Mark, 6" **$15-$18**
Right: **227** Japan, 4.5" **$12-$15**

Left: **228** No Mark, 4.5" **$10-$12**
Center: **229** E-3980, 6" **$12-$15**
Right: **230** No Mark, 4.75" **$10-$12**

Left: **231** Inarco E-3272, 3.5" **$15-$18**
Center: **232** Rubens 472, 5" **$15-$18**
Right: **233** Inarco E-3272, 3.5" **$15-$18**

Left: **234** No Mark, 5" **$12-$15**
Right: **235** Japan, 4.75" **$15-$18**

Left: **236** No Mark, 5.5" **$10-$12**
Center: **237** Japan, 5" **$15-$18**
Right: **238** Ucagco Ceramic Co, 5.25" **$15-$18**

239 No Mark, 5.75" **$18-$20**

240 Japan, 5.5" **$18-$20**

Left: **241** Grantcrest Japan, Wall Pocket, 6" **$15-$18**
Center: **242** Rubens 587, 6.25" **$15-$18**
Right: **243** Inarco E-3775, 6" **$15-$18**

Left: **244** Napcoware C-6434, 5.5" **$15-$18**
Right: **245** Napcoware C-6434, 5.5" **$15-$18**

Left: **246** Royal Sealy 6812, Japan, 5,75" **$12-$15**
Right: **247** Royal Sealy 6812, Japan, 5.75" **$12-$15**

Left: **248** Relpo 6529, 6.5" **$15-$18**
Center: **249** Rubens 4101, 5.75" **$15-$18**
Right: **250** Relpo 6529, 6.5" **$15-$18**

Left: **251** Caffco Japan E-3147, 6.5" **$15-$18**
Center: **252** Caffco Japan, 6" **$12-$15**
Right: **253** Japan 1524, 6" **$12-$15**

Left: **254** 6094, 5.5" **$18-$20**
Right: **255** Napcoware C-8825, 5" **$18-$20**

Left: **256** No Mark, 5" **$18-$20**
Center: **257** No Mark, 5" **$18-$20**
Right: **258** Japan, Wall Pocket, 5.5" **$20-$22**

Left: **259** Japan, 6" **$15-$18**
Center: **260** Relpo 6434, 6" **$12-$15**
Right: **261** Japan 7851, 7" **$15-$18**

262 1956, Napco C1839B, 8.25" **$20-$22**

263 Japan, Wall Pocket, 6.5" **$20-$22**

Left: **264** Norcrest Japan, 6" **$12-$15**
Right: **265** Rubens 3215A, 5.25" **$12-$15**

Left: **266** No Mark, 5.25" **$18-$20**
Right: **267** 1961, Relpo 5137A, 5" **$18-$20**

268 S679A, 5.5" **$12-$15**

Christmas

The Christmas planters are appealing to collectors and non-collectors alike, for they make a colorful addition to standard holiday decorations. The meticulous attention to detail and careful painting found in the earlier vases cannot be duplicated at a reasonable price in this age of mass production. The lovely ladies in their bright holiday clothing are becoming difficult to find and prices are rising as more collectors come to realize their worth. Watch for accessories such as candleholders and salt and pepper shakers that match some of the vases.

Left: **269** Napcoware X-6047, 3.25" **$5-$6**
Center: **270** Napcoware X-6051, 4.75" **$12-$15**
Right: **271** Napcoware X-6047, 3.25" **$5-$6**

Left: **272** No Mark, 4.5" **$12-$15**
Center: **273** Inarco, 6" **$15-$18**
Right: **274** Japan, 5" **$12-$15**

Left: **275** Napcoware X-8995, 5.5" **$15-$18**
Right: **276** Japan, Wall Pocket, 5.75" **$20-$22**

Left: **277** Napco X-6389, 5.25" **$15-$18**
Center: **278** Giftwares Japan, 4" **$10-$12**
Right: **279** No Mark, 5.5" **$12-$15**

Left: **280** Napcoware X-7260, 5.75" **$18-$20**
Center: **281** Relpo 6024, 7" **$20-$22**
Right: **282** 9706, 4" **$10-$12**

Left: **283** X-8370, 5.5" **$18-$20**
Right: **284** No Mark, 3" **$10-$12**

Left: **285** No Mark, 4.25" **$15-$18**
Center: **286** 1959, Napco CX4552, 6" **$40-$45**
Right: **287** No Mark, 4.25" **$15-$18**

288 Napco, 4" **$15-$18**

Left: **289** Napcoware X-8791, 8" **$20-$22**
Center: **290** Napcoware X-8790, 6" **$15-$18**
Right: **291** Napcoware X-8787, Candleholder, 3.5" **$10-$12**

292 Fine A Quality, 7" **$18-$20**

Left: **293** 1959 Holt Howard, 5" **$18-$20**
Center: **294** Japan, 5.25" **$15-$18**
Right: **295** Napcoware 9756, 4" **$12-$18**

Left: **296** Japan, 5.25" **$10-$12**
Center: **297** No Mark, 5.25" **$12-$15**
Right: **298** Ucagco China Co., Vase and Candleholder, 4.5" **$15-$18**

Left: **299** Napcoware 1CX2403, 5.5" **$35-$40**
Right: **300** Napcoware 1CX2403, 5.5" **$35-$40**

Left: **301** No Mark, 5.75" **$12-$15**
Center: **302** Lefton 3104, 5.5" **$15-$18**
Right: **303** Inarco E4446, 6" **$18-$20**

Left: **304** Napco S715B, 5" **$12-$15**
Right: **305** Nancy Pew 2378, 4.5" **$10-$12**

Left: **306** Relpo A916, 4.5" **$15-$18**
Center: **307** FF, 5.75" **$12-$15**
Right: **308** SSCO, 4" **$10-$12**

309 1964, Samson Import Co,
Relpo 5592, 8" **$25-$30**

Left: **310** No Mark, 6.5" **$22-$25**
Center: **311** Napco AX2752A, 7" **$25-$28**
Right: **312** R/B Japan 1213, 6.75" **$22-$25**

Left: **313** No Mark, 6" **$15-$18**
Center: **314** 1959, Napco CX3811C, 6.5" **$18-$20**
Right: **315** Dickson, "Nodder", 7" **$30-$35**

Left: **316** 1962, Napco, Bedford Ohio, Hand Painted, CX-5478, 6.5" **$22-$25**
Right: **317** l962, Napco, Bedford Ohio, Hand Painted, CX-5478, 6.5" **$22-$25**

Left: **318** NOEL Japan, 4" **$12-$15**
Right: **319** S268, 4.75" **$18-$20**

Left: **320** 1956, Napco AX-2193B, 7" **$30-$35**
Center: **321** 1956, Napco AX-2193B, 7" **$30-$35**
Right: **322** 1956, Napco AX-2193C, 7" **$30-$35**

Left: **323** Napcoware X7261, 7" **$25-$30**
Center: **324** Napcoware X6966, 7.5" **$30-$35**
Right: **325** Napcoware X7261, 7" **$25-$30**

Left: **326** 1957, Napco CX2679A, 5.5" **$18-$20**
Center: **327** Relpo Japan, 6.5" **$20-$22**
Right: **328** 1960, Napco CX4828C, 5.75" **$20-$22**

Left: **329** 1960, Samson Import Co, Relpo 456L, 6" **$22-$25**
Right: **330** 1960, Samson Import Co, Relpo 456S, 4" **$18-$20**

Left: **331** Napco 4JX4092, 5" **$22-$25**
Center: **332** 1963, Inarco E-1133, 5.5" **$22-$25**
Right: **333** Thames Japan, 5" **$22-$25**

Left: **334** Napco K2568, 6" **$18-$20**
Right: **335** Giftwares Japan, 4.75" **$15-$18**

Left: **336** Hobnail Hollyware, 4.25" **$22-$25**
Center: **337** No Mark, 6" **$20-$22**
Right: **338** HF Co P632, Japan, 5" **$15-$18**

Left: **339** Napcoware X-8390, 7" **$25-$28**
Center: **340** Napcoware X-8389, 6" **$22-$25**
Right: **341** Napcoware X-8388, Candleholder, 4" **$18-$20**

342 Relpo SW888, 8" **$40-$45**

Left: **343** Napco S47, 6" **$10-$12**
Center: **344** No Mark, 5" **$10-$12**
Right: **345** Napco S925, 6" **$12-$15**

Left: **346** Country Store Products, Japan, 6" **$12-$15**
Right: **347** Inarco E-4528, 7" **$15-$18**

Left: **348** HF Co P617A, Japan, 4.25" **$18-$20**
Right: **349** Napco S716A, 4" **$12-15**

350 1963, Samson Import Co, Relpo 5460, Electrified, 8" **$40-$45**

Left: **351** Napco, 3.5" **$18-$20**
Center: **352** Napco S1699, 7" **$20-$22**
Right: **353** Napco 1CX4182, 5" **$20-$22**

Left: **354** Napco 1TX4568/S, 2.5" **$8-$10**
Center: **355** X-7976, 4" **$10-$12**
Right: **356** Napcoware X-8404, 3" **$8-$10**

Left: **357** Relpo A1098, 5.5" **$20-$22**
Center: **358** 1963, Inarco E-1134, 5.75" **$20-$22**
Right: **359** No Mark, 5.25" **$18-$20**

Left: **360** Relpo 6573, 5.25" **$10-$12**
Right: **361** Relpo 6573, 5" **$10-$12**

Left: **362** 1956, Napco AX1690PC, 5.25" **$20-$22**
Center: **363** Relpo A-1484, 7.5" **$28-$30**
Right: **364** 1956, Napco AX1690PC, 5.25" **$20-$22**

Left: **365** No Mark, 4.5" **$12-$15**
Center: **366** Ucagco China Co, 5.25" **$12-$15**
Right: **367** No Mark, 5" **$12-$15**

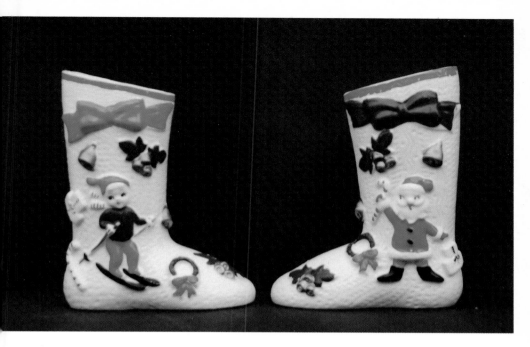

Left: **368** Ucagco China Co, 6.5" **$15-$18**
Right: **369** Ucagco China Co, 6.5" **$15-$18**

370 2136, 4.5" **$10-$12**

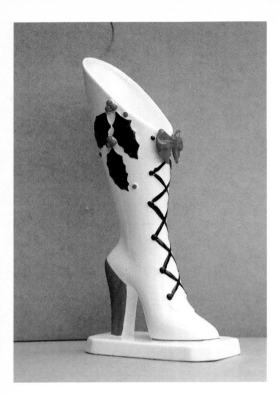

371 Napco S486A, 11" **$15-$18**

372 1960, Napco AX4695, H.Unisuo, 4.25" **$15-$18**

Left: **373** Napcoware 1998, 4.25" **$10-$12**
Right: **374** Napcoware X-8659, 4.25" **$10-$12**

Left: **375** RR Imports Japan, 7" **$12-$15**
Right: **376** Lefton 2915, 4.5" **$12-$15**

Left: **377** Napco 1LX931, 4.5" **$12-$15**
Center: **378** Rubens 6172, 5.25" **$15-$18**
Right: **379** Lefton 2306, 4.25" **$10-$12**

Clowns

Bring on the clowns in all their glory! They inject a bright note in a figural planter collection and are vastly appealing. I buy every one I can find, for I love their whimsical appeal. Sometimes they can be found incorporated into the blue and pink design of the baby planters, for clowns really are for children. However, I suspect quite a few grown-ups are enthralled by them, as well.

380 No Mark, 5" **$25-$28**

Left: **381** Rubens 388X, 7" **$20-$22**
Right: **382** Rubens 4150, 6" **$15-$18**

Left: **383** No Mark, 5" **$18-$20**
Right: **384** Napco 734, 4.25" **$12-$15**

Left: **385** Patmar Japan, 5" **$15-$18**
Right: **386** Inarco E-5150, 6" **$22-$25**

Left: **387** No Mark, 5" **$15-$18**
Right: **388** No Mark, 5" **$15-$18**

389 Enesco E-7297, 7" **$15-$18**

Left: **390** 1987, Nancy Pew 8304, Japan, 6" **$12-$15**
Right: **391** Inarco E-1683, 6" **$20-$22**

Left: **392** Inarco, 5.75" **$15-$18**
Center: **393** Nancy Pew, 7.25" **$15-$18**
Right: **394** Inarco SB-2026, 4.5" **$12-$15**

Left: **395** Relpo 6777, 6" **$15-$18**
Right: **396** Napcoware 3321, 5.5" **$15-$18**

397 Shafford YONA Original 1957,
Wall Pocket, 7.5" **$30-$35**

Left: **398** No Mark, Wall Pocket, 7" **$28-$30**
Right: **399** No Mark, Wall Pocket, 7" **$28-$30**

Easter

From yellow chicks to pink and white bunnies, the Easter planters are very attractive. Not as plentiful as the Christmas or Valentine vases, it is still possible to acquire a nice collection at reasonable prices. They make excellent holiday decorations, filled with colored Easter eggs to show them off at their best.

Left: **400** E-4650, 7.5" **$18-$20**
Right: **401** Inarco E-4684, 8.75" **$18-$20**

Left: **402** No Mark, 4" **$10-$12**
Center: **403** No Mark, 5.5" **$15-$18**
Right: **404** No Mark, 5" **$10-$12**

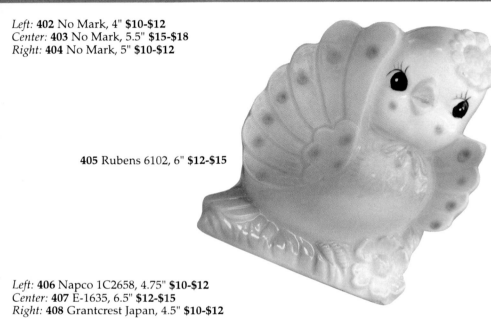

405 Rubens 6102, 6" **$12-$15**

Left: **406** Napco 1C2658, 4.75" **$10-$12**
Center: **407** E-1635, 6.5" **$12-$15**
Right: **408** Grantcrest Japan, 4.5" **$10-$12**

Left: **409** 4423, 7" **$12-$15**
Center: **410** No Mark, 5.5" **$12-$15**
Right: **411** Lefton 2962, 6.5" **$12-$15**

Left: **412** No Mark, 4" **$10-$12**
Center: **413** No Mark, 6" **$12-$15**
Right: **414** Lefton 1439, 4.25" **$12-$15**

Left: **415** Napco 4297, 6.5" **$12-$15**
Right: **416** 57336, 5.5" **$10-$12**

Left: **417** Napcoware C-6903, 5.5" **$12-$15**
Center: **418** Japan JN-4080, 6" **$12-$15**
Right: **419** Relpo A867, 5" **$12-$15**

Left: **420** 6106, 5" **$8-$10**
Right: **421** 6106, 5" **$8-$10**

422 Lefton KW2925, 6" **$10-$12**

Left: **423** Rubens 342, Japan, 5" **$12-$15**
Right: **424** No Mark, 4.5" **$12-$15**

Lovely Ladies

One of the most collectible of all the categories, these beautifully dressed ladies will brighten your shelves. They are fairly easy to find and are so well designed they could be used to add a touch of color to any room setting. I especially love to see the little gold slippers peeking out from voluminous skirts, as well as the gorgeous outfits worn by some of the ladies. Head vase aficionados have already started adding them to their collections and, although not a head vase in the true sense of the word, they are, none the less, a highly desirable companion collectible.

Left: **425** Lefton "Olive" 1685B, 6" **$15-$18**
Center: **426** No Mark, 7" **$20-$22**
Right: **427** 1962, Samson Import Co 5380, 5.75" **$18-$20**

Left: **428** CalArt Ceramics, Japan, 6" **$15-$18**
Center: **429** No Mark, 4.5" **$12-$15**
Right: **430** CalArt Ceramics, Japan, 6" **$15-$18**

Left: **431** No Mark, 7" **$18-$20**
Right: **432** No Mark, 7" **$18-$20**

Left: **433** Napcoware C-6364, 5.75", **$15-$18**
Center: **434** No Mark, 6" **$18-$20**
Right: **435** Napcoware C-5622, 5.5" **$15-$18**

Left: **436** Japan, 6.5" **$20-$22**
Center: **437** Velco 3184, 6.75" **$22-$25**
Right: **438** No Mark, 7" **$22-$25**

Left: **439** No Mark, 7" **$22-$25**
Right: **440** No Mark, 7" **$22-$25**

Left: **441** Napcoware, 6" **$15-$18**
Center: **442** Rubens 158, 6.25" **$15-$18**
Right: **443** Napcoware, 6" **$15-$18**

Left: **444** Rubens 464M, 5.5" **$15-$18**
Center: **445** No Mark, 6" **$18-$20**
Right: **446** Inarco E-871, 5.75" **$15-$18**

Left: **447** E-3146 Japan, 6.5" **$20-$22**
Center: **448** Napcoware C-6435, 6" **$18-$20**
Right: **449** A-110, 6.5" **$20-$22**

Left: **450** 6094, 7" **$18-$20**
Center: **451** Japan 2180, 8" **$20-$22**
Right: **452** 6094, 7" **$18-$20**

Left: **453** Inarco E-436, 5.75" **$15-$18**
Center: **454** Inarco E-2317, 5.25" **$15-$18**
Right: **455** Inarco E-436, 5.75" **$15-$18**

Left: **456** R/B Japan, 8" **$30-$35**
Right: **457** 1355, 8" **$30-$35**

Left: **458** Relpo 6081, 6.25" **$15-$18**
Center: **459** C-8548, 5.75" **$15-$18**
Right: **460** Relpo 6081, 6.25" **$15-$18**

Left: **461** No Mark, 6" **$12-$15**
Center: **462** Relpo 6447, 8" **$25-$28**
Right: **463** No Mark, 6" **$12-$15**

Left: **464** Lefton 290B, 8" **$30-$35**
Right: **465** Lefton 535A, 8" **$30-$35**

Left: **466** Nancy Pew Japan, 7.5" **$25-$28**
Right: **467** R/B Japan, 8.25" **$30-$35**

Left: **468** No Mark, 7" **$20-$22**
Center: **469** No Mark, 7.75" **$28-$30**
Right: **470** No Mark, 6.5" **$20-$22**

Left: **471** No Mark, 6.25" **$25-$28**
Center: **472** Giftwares Japan, 7" **$28-$30**
Right: **473** No Mark, 6.25" **$22-$25**

Left: **474** No Mark, 8" **$25-$28**
Right: **475** Inarco E-2447, 5.25" **$18-$20**

476 No Mark, 7.25" **$28-$30**

Left: **477** C-6362, 5.5" **$25-$28**
Center: **478** 1960, Samson Import Co, Relpo 5117B, 5" **$25-$28**
Right: **479** Nanco Products, Boston, Japan, 5.25" **$22-$25**

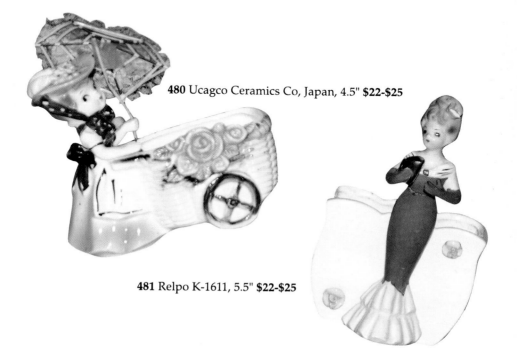

480 Ucagco Ceramics Co, Japan, 4.5" **$22-$25**

481 Relpo K-1611, 5.5" **$22-$25**

Masculine

Fishing is by far the most popular pastime depicted on these planters with a masculine theme, and were no doubt popular Father's Day gifts. The barbershop quartet planters are not found in any great number, but make a wonderful addition to a collection. Throw in a train engine or a stagecoach, a boat or a gypsy wagon, perhaps an automobile or two, and the man of the house is well on his way to an outstanding collection.

482 Relpo 5546, 5.75" **$22-$25**

Left: **483** Inarco E-4303, 6" **$18-$20**
Right: **484** Inarco E-4303, 6" **$18-$20**

Left: **485** 1958, Samson Import Co 359A, 5" **$25-$28**
Right: **486** No Mark, 6.5" **$28-$30**

Left: **487** E O Brody Co 05071, Japan, 6.25" **$10-$12**
Center: **488** 1958, Samson Import Co, Relpo P-121, 6.25" **$12-$15**
Right: **489** 1962, Inarco E-467, 3.75" **$12-$15**

490 4954, 5" **$12-$15**

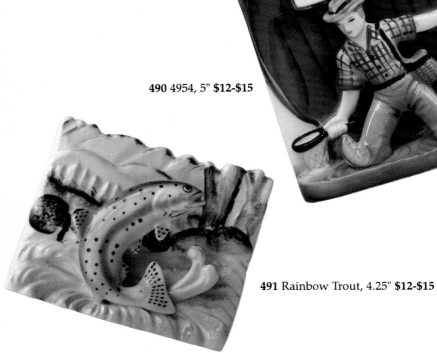

491 Rainbow Trout, 4.25" **$12-$15**

Left: **492** Nancy Pew Japan, 3.75" **$10-$12**
Right: **493** Nancy Pew Japan, 3.75" **$10-$12**

Left: **494** Rubens 5215, 7" **$12-$15**
Right: **495** Napco K3186, Wall Pocket, 4" **$18-$20**

Left: **496** Lefton 1094, 4.25" **$10-$12**
Right: **497** 1956, Napco K-1905, 4.75" **$12-$15**

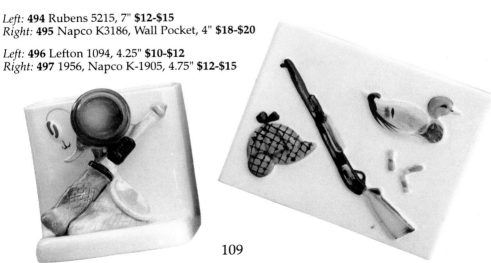

Left: **498** Rubens 397, 6" **$15-$18**
Right: **499** Relpo 6044, 6.25" **$12-$15**

500 No Mark, 4.5" **$10-$12**

501 Inarco, 4" **$10-$12**

Left: **502** No Mark, 4.5" **$10-$12**
Center: **503** Relpo, 6.5" **$12-$15**
Right: **504** Inarco, 4" **$10-$12**

Left: **505** Enesco, 4.5" **$12-$15**
Right: **506** Shafford, 4.25" **$12-$15**

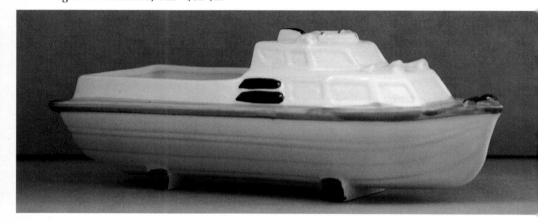

507 Rubens 5149, 3.5" **$10-$12**

Left: **508** Lefton 04519, 4.5" **$8-$10**
Right: **509** 1984, Lefton 04519, 4.5" **$8-$10**

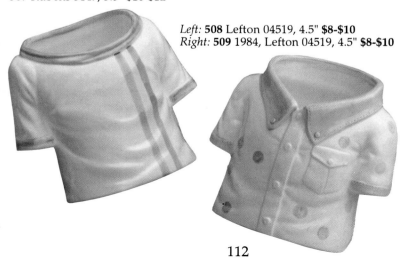

Miscellaneous

Some planters are too few in number to be included in a special category, and thus are relegated to this miscellaneous section, even though there are some outstanding examples shown here which deserve recognition in their own right. The Halloween Jack-O-Lantern shown is very rare; it has cut-outs in the back for inserting a light. Anything Halloween is hard to find. Except for turkey planters, Thanksgiving is not well represented. Mother's Day planters are not easily found but any of the vases in the Lovely Ladies section could be used for this purpose. St. Patrick's Day vases are hard to find; graduation, retirement, get well and friendship planters are scarce.

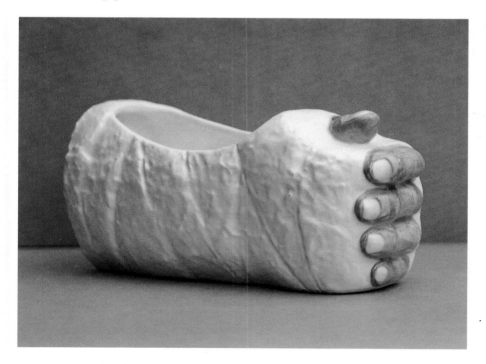

510 Inarco, 3.5" **$10-$12**

Left: **511** No Mark, 6.5" **$12-$15**
Right: **512** Inarco E-5082, 5.75" **$15-$18**

513 Lefton 4292, 7" **$20-$22**

Left: **514** Rubens 1966 Japan, 6.5" **$18-$20**
Right: **515** Rubens 1966 Japan, 6.5" **$18-$20**

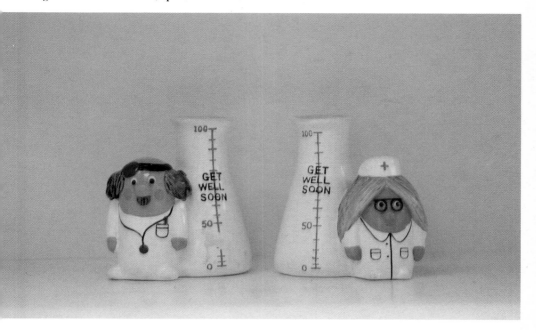

Left: **516** 1978, Enesco, 3.5" **$8-$10**
Right: **517** 1978, Enesco, 3.5" **$8-$10**

Left: **518** Holland Floral, 6" **$10-$12**
Center: **519** Nancy Pew 4120, Japan, 6" **$12-$15**
Right: **520** Relpo, 5" **$10-$12**

Left: **521** Relpo 5503, 4.5" **$10-$12**
Center: **522** Relpo 5984, 6" **$18-$20**
Right: **523** Japan 6144, 5" **$10-$12**

Left: **524** Rubens 9852, 6.75" **$12-$15**
Center: **525** A-352, Vase and Candleholder, 5.25" **$12-$15**
Right: **526** Midwest Importers, 6.75" **$12-$15**

Left: **527** 1961, Samson Import Co 5105A, 6" **$20-$22**
Right: **528** 1960, Samson Import Co 5105B, 6" **$20-$22**

529 Napcoware C-8184, 5.5" **$28-$30**

Left: **530** 1964, Sampson Import Co, Relpo 5367, 6" **$35-$40**
Right: **531** Napco S633, 4.5" **$25-28**

Left: **532** Lefton 6400, 6.5" **$30-$35**
Right: **533** No Mark, 5.5" **$28-$30**

Left: **534** No Mark, 6" **$18-$20**
Center: **535** R/B Japan 2708, 4" **$10-$12**
Right: **536** Relpo A-1992, 5.5" **$18-$20**

537 Napco C-6847, 7" **$15-$18**

Left: **538** No Mark, 5" **$15-$18**
Center: **539** Thames 9211, 7" **$22-$25**
Right: **540** No Mark, 5" **$20-$22**

541 Japan, 6.5" **$30-$35**

Left: **542** Royal Japan, 4.75" **$20-$22**
Center: **543** No Mark, 5" **$30-$35**
Right: **544** Japan, 5.5" **$28-$30**

545 Napcoware C5528, 5.25" **$30-$35**

546 Inarco E-2226, Wall Pocket, 6" **$18-$20**

Left: **547** Lefton 710, 4.5" **$12-$15**
Right: **548** Consco Japan, 4" **$15-$18**

549 No Mark, 6.5" **$28-$30**

Left: **550** J5296, 4.5" **$15-$18**
Right: **551** Lefton 4647, 4" **$12-$15**

552 1963, Samson Import Co, Relpo 5461B, 6" **$20-$22**

553 Inarco E-4299, 5.75" **$12-$15**

556 Relpo A-1349, 5.25" **$10-$12**

Left: **554** 5573, 8" **$20-$22**
Right: **555** Temple Treasures, F.N.
Kistner Co, 50214, 5" **$18-$20**

557 Lefton 4698, 6" **$12-$15**

Nursery Rhymes and Fairy Tales

A favorite category of mine, although in rather short supply. The Old Woman in a Shoe shown spanking one of her many children is an outstanding example of the magnificent detail of some of these planters. It is a marvel that these vases were produced at such a low cost that they could be used for inexpensive floral arrangements, considering the exquisite workmanship that went into some of them. Be aware that there are also figurines and salt and pepper shakers that are a match for the nursery rhyme characters and that many of the vases also come in two different sizes.

Left: **558** Florart China, 4" **$12-$15**
Center: **559** Enesco Japan, 8" **$30-35**
Right: **560** No Mark, 3" **$12-$15**

Left: **561** No Mark, 5.75" **$18-$20**
Center: **562** Inarco E-5153, 6.25" **$18-$20**
Right: **563** No Mark, 5.75" **$18-$20**

Left: **564** 1956 Napco A1721D, Little
    Miss Muffet, 7" **$28-$30**
Right: **565** 1956 Napco A1492D, Little
    Miss Muffet, Figurine, 5" **$20-$22**

Left: **566** Japan, Shaker, 2.5" **$8-$10**
Center left: **567** Lefton 5881N, 5" **$30-$35**
Center right: **568** Lefton AR5882, 4" **$25-$28**
Right: **569** Japan, Shaker, 2.5" **$8-$10**

Left: **570** Parma A-525, 6" **$28-$30**
Right: **571** Parma A-525, 6" **$28-$30**

Left: **572** No Mark, 5.75" **$28-$30**
Center: **573** Inarco CB-2025, 5.5" **$28-$30**
Right: **574** No Mark, 5.5" **$28-$30**

Left: **575** Napco 1LX4301/S, 5" **$30-$35**
Right: **576** 798, 4.5" **$28-$30**

Left: **577** No Mark, 4" **$12-$15**
Center: **578** Japan, 4" **$12-$15**
Right: **579** No Mark, 4" **$12-$15**

Left: **580** Relco, Shaker, 4" **$10-$12**
Center: **581** 1956, Napco A1721C, Little Bo Peep, 7" **$30-$3**
Right: **582** Relco, Shaker, 4" **$10-$12**

Left: **583** 1956, Napco A1720E, Goldilocks, 5.25" **$25-$28**
Center: **584** 1956, Napco A1493D, 4.5" **$25-$28**
Right: **585** 1956, Napco A1720B, Alice in Wonderland, 5.25" **$25-$28**

590 Relpo A918, 7" **$30-$35**

Left: **586** Relco, Shaker, 4" **$10-$12**
Center left: **587** Relco, Shaker, 4" **$10-$12**
Center right: **588** 1956, Napco 1721F, Queen
of Hearts, 7.25" **$30-$35**
Right: **589** Napco A1943, Figurine, 4.5" **$25-$28**

Left: **591** 1956, Napco A1720A, Little Red Riding Hood, 5" **$25-$28**
Center: **592** No Mark, 4.25" **$25-$28**
Right: **593** No Mark, 5.25" **$25-$28**

595 Napco S5578, 4.25" **$25-$28**

594 E O Brody Co 05041, 5.25" **$20-$22**

Left: **596** K-2289, 6" **$15-$18**
Center: **597** Napco, 5" **$12-$15**
Right: **598** R/B Japan, 5" **$12-$15**

Raggedy Ann and Andy

One of the most appealing of all the categories, you'll find you can't have just one. For every Raggedy Ann there is an Andy to match, and it takes a great deal of searching to find the pair. It is also difficult to find planters that do not have at least some flaking of the red paint, but they are easily put back together again with a paint brush and a steady hand. Beware of the Raggedy disease which entices you to buy not only vases, but lamps, dishes, sheets, curtains, lunchboxes, and the most amazing assortment of associated paraphernalia.

Left: **599** 1976, The Bobbs Merrill Co, Rubens 4185, 6" **$30-$35**
Center: **600** 1976, The Bobbs Merrill Co, Rubens 4186, 5" **$28-$30**
Right: **601** Inarco, 5.75" **$25-$28**

Left: **602** 1976, The Bobbs Merrill Co, Rubens 4188, 6" **$30-$35**
Right: **603** 1976, The Bobbs Merrill Co, Rubens 4188, 6" **$30-$35**

Left: **604** 1976, The Bobbs Merrill Co, Rubens 4192, 6.25" **$28-$30**
Center: **605** Relpo 6493, 5" **$28-$30**
Right: **606** Relpo 6667, 6" **$28-$30**

Left: **607** No Mark, 6" **$22-$25**
Center: **608** 1976, The Bobbs Merrill Co, Rubens 4180, 5" **$28-$30**
Right: **609** Relpo 6462, 5.5" **$22-$25**

Left: **610** C-8794, 5" **$18-$20**
Center: **611** Inarco E-4272, 6" **$18-$20**
Right: **612** Napcoware 9138, 5" **$18-$20**

Left: **613** Inarco E-6229, 5.5" **$15-$18**
Center left: **614** Inarco E-6229, 5.5" **$15-$18**
Center right: **615** No Mark, 5" **$15-$18**
Right: **616** No Mark, 5" **$15-$18**

Left: **617** Rubens 4149, 6" **$20-$22**
Center: **618** 1976, The Bobbs Merrill Co, Rubens PC-9389, 5.75" **$18-$20**
Right: **619** No Mark, 6" **$18-$20**

Left: **620** Rubens 4016, 4.25" **$20-$22**
Right: **621** 1976, The Bobbs Merrill Co, Rubens 4193, 4.5" **$25-$28**

Left: **625** 1976, The Bobbs Merrill Co,
Rubens 4181, 5.5" **$28-$30**
Right: **626** 1976, The Bobbs Merrill Co,
Rubens 4181, 5.5" **$28-$30**

Left: **622** Japan, 5.75" **$18-$20**
Center: **623** Rubens 3236, Musical, 8" **$30-$35**
Right: **624** No Mark, 5.75" **$18-$20**

Left: **627** Rubens 4109, 6" **$25-$28**
Right: **628** Rubens 4109, 6" **$25-$28**

Left: **629** Rubens 4149X, Japan, 6" **$25-$28**
Right: **630** Rubens 4149X, Japan, 6" **$25-$28**

Left: **631** Rubens 4016, 4" **$22-$25**
Right: **632** Rubens 4016, 4" **$22-$25**

Left: **633** Nancy Pew Japan, 6" **$22-$25**
Center: **634** No Mark, 5.5" **$12-$15**
Right: **635** Price Imports, 6.25" **$20-$22**

Left: **636** Ardco, 6.25" **$18-$20**
Right: **637** Lefton 6921, 6.5" **$20-$22**

Left: **638** A / 524S, 6.5" **$20-$22**
Right: **639** Ardco Japan, 6.5" **$20-$22**

Left: **640** Napcoware C-9081,
6" **$25-$28**
Right: **641** Napcoware C-9081,
6" **$25-$28**

Left: **642** Relpo 6465, 6" **$25-$28**
Right: **643** Relpo 6465, 6" **$25-$28**

Religious

From a beautiful Madonna to an Infant of Prague, there are many wonderful planters to be found with a religious theme. The Madonnas are plentiful but prices tend to be high because of their exposure in the lady head vase price guides. The larger and more ornate the planter is, the more expensive it will be. The First Communion planter shown is a rare find, a real gem to add to a collection, as is the bride and groom planter with which it is pictured.

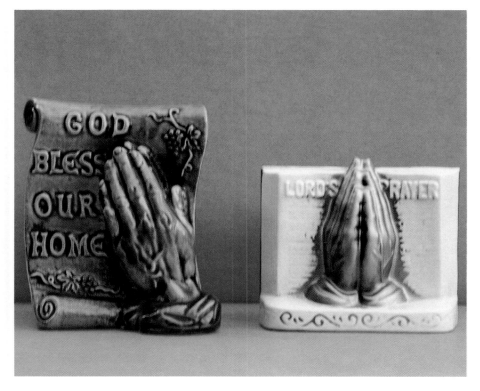

Left: **644** Enesco E-7284, 5.5" **$10-$12**
Right: **645** Rubens 103, 4" **$10-$12**

Left: **646** 1958, Samson Import Co 357B, 5.25" **$15-$18**
Right: **647** R/B Japan, 6.5" **$20-$22**

Left: **648** No Mark, 6" **$20-$22**
Center: **649** No Mark, 8.5" **$20-$22**
Right: **650** No Mark, 6.5" **$25-$28**

Left: **651** 1959, Napco C3810B, 4" **$18-$20**
Right: **652** Relpo A1608, 6" **$20-$22**

Left: **653** 5B/401, 5.25" **$12-$15**
Center: **654** Lego Japan, 8.5" **$30-$35**
Right: **655** No Mark, 5.25" **$12-$15**

Left: **656** Japan, 7.5" **$28-$30**
Center: **657** Inarco E-2588, 11.5" **$18-$20**
Right: **658** Norcrest Japan E-680, 7.5" **$20-$22**

Left: **659** Inarco E-3789, 5.75" **$15-$18**
Center: **660** Lefton 1749, 8.5" **$28-$30**
Right: **661** Relpo 6637, 6" **$15-$18**

Left: **662** No Mark, 5" **$15-$18**
Center: **663** No Mark, 7.25" **$28-$30**
Right: **664** No Mark, 5.75" **$18-$20**

665 Napcoware R-6070, 12" **$30-$35**

Left: **666** No Mark, 5.5" **$25-$28**
Center: **667** Relpo SW1020, 6.75" **$25-$28**
Right: **668** Nancy Pew Japan, 4.25" **$20-$22**

Left: **669** E-370, 7" **$30-$35**
Right: **670** 4352, 6" **$30-$35**

Left: **671** Japan, 5.75" **$15-$18**
Center: **672** No Mark, 7.5" **$20-$22**
Right: **673** Napco S1717, 5" **$18-$20**

Left: **674** Japan, 6.5" **$15-$18**
Center: **675** Napco S175, 5.75" **$15-$18**
Right: **676** Napcoware, 6.5" **$18-$20**

Left: **677** Japan, 4.75" **$20-$22**
Right: **678** No Mark, 5.5" **$22-$25**

Left: **679** No Mark, 4" **$15-$18**
Center: **680** Fine A Quality, 5.5" **$15-$18**
Right: **681** Fine A Quality, 4" **$15-$18**

Left: **682** No Mark, 5" **$28-$30**
Right: **683** 1959, Napco C3813, 5.5" **$25-$28**

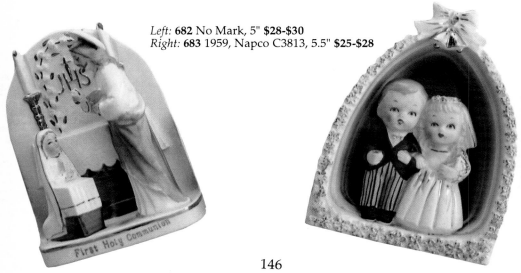

First Holy Communion

146

684 Rubens 318, Japan, 9" **$30-$35**

Left: **685** 6A/420, 5.25" **$12-$15**
Center: **686** S285A, 4.5" **$18-$20**
Right: **687** 6A400, 5" **$10-$12**

688 No Mark, 5" **$15-$18**

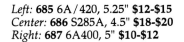

689 Inarco 4J3757/P,
8" **$18-$20**

Left: **690** 63, Wall Pocket, 3.5" **$10-$12**
Right: **691** Lefton 50427, Wall Pocket, 4" **$10-$12**

Sports

Golf-related planters seem to be the most prevalent in the sports category, although baseball and football are not far behind. Even some of the baby planters have sports themes, as evidenced by the number of "new rookie" vases to be found; perhaps a little wishful thinking on the part of the new father. Many times planters can fit into more than one category, such as the baby and children planters which also have a sports theme, making it difficult to decide in which section to place them.

Left: **692** Napcoware 9262, 6.25" **$18-$20**
Right: **693** Napcoware 9262, 6.25" **$18-$20**

694 Lefton, 7.25" **$20-$22**

Left: **695** 1962, Samson Import Co, Relpo 413A, 6" **$15-$18**
Right: **696** 125, 5.5" **$15-$18**

150

Left: **697** Napcoware 125, 5" **$15-$18**
Center: **698** Inarco E-3172, 6" **$18-$20**
Right: **699** Relpo 6558, 4.5" **$10-$12**

Left: **700** Rubens 593BB, 5.25" **$15-$18**
Center: **701** Rubens 436, 5.25" **$15-$18**
Right: **702** Rubens 641, 5" **$15-$18**

Left: **703** Napcoware C-8221, 5.5" **$12-$15**
Center: **704** E-4372, 6.5" **$12-$15**
Right: **705** Napcoware 8223, 5.5" **$12-$15**

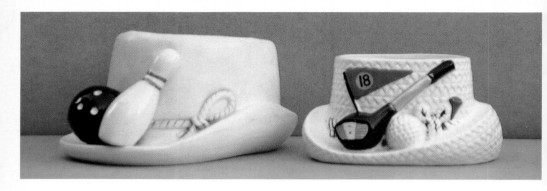

Left: **706** Lefton, 4" **$10-$12**
Right: **707** Rubens 439, 3" **$10-$12**

Left: **708** API Japan, 5.5" **$8-$10**
Center: **709** Napco K-2642, 3.5" **$10-$12**
Right: **710** 1967, Samson Import Co, Relpo 5151, 4.75" **$8-$10**

Left: **711** Japan 2198, 4" **$8-$10**
Center: **712** No Mark, 5.25" **$15-$18**
Right: **713** Inarco, 4.5" **$10-$12**

Left: **714** Lefton H-8085, 5" **$12-$15**
Right: **715** Rubens Taiwan, 4.75" **$6-$8**

Left: **716** Napcoware C-6072, 6" **$12-$15**
Right: **717** Japan 55-124, 3" **$12-$15**

Left: **718** No Mark, 5" **$8-$10**
Right: **719** Napcoware C-7315, 6" **$8-$10**

Left: **720** Napcoware C-6415, 5.5" **$12-$15**
Right: **721** Relpo 6881, 5.5" **$12-$15**

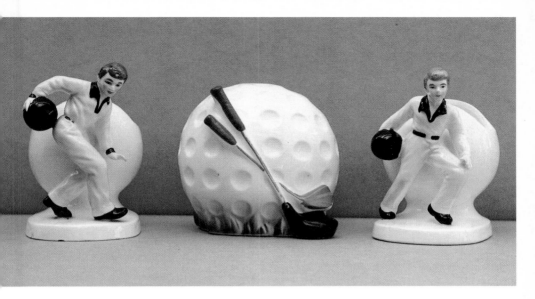

Left: **722** 1960, Samson Import Co 3288, 5.25" **$12-$15**
Center: **723** Inarco E-4130, 5" **$10-$12**
Right: **724** 1962, Samson Import Co, Relpo 5308, 5.25" **$12-$15**

Left: **725** Rubens 5137X, 4" **$10-$12**
Center: **726** Relpo, 4" **$12-$15**
Right: **727** SX1759, 2 piece set, 3.75" **$12-$15**

Left: **728** Japan, 6.25" **$18-$20**
Center: **729** Japan OR 5367, 5.5" **$18-$20**
Right: **730** Inarco E-3219, 5.5" **$18-$20**

Left: **731** Japan, 6" **$18-$20**
Right: **732** Napcoware, 3" **$8-$10**

Left: **733** Inarco, 3" **$8-$10**
Right: **734** Napcoware C-8450, 3.25" **$8-$10**

735 C-9608, 4.5" **$10-$12**

736 Napco K5443, 5" **$10-$12**

Valentines

Don't you love the ladies with their dresses and fancy bonnets trimmed with hearts? It is difficult to make a choice between the brightly decorated ladies and the beautiful children, so why not collect them all! You will encounter more of the heart-shaped vases, either plain or with trimming, than the more desirable ladies and children, but a nice collection is not difficult to acquire.

Left: **737** R/B Japan 1414, 8" **$25-$28**
Right: **738** Relpo A-1840, 7" **$25-$28**

739 R/B Japan, 5.75" **$22-$25**

741 Rubens 6152V, 7.25" **$22-$25**

740 Rubens 142V, 7" **$25-$28**

742 No Mark, 5.5" **$20-$22**

Left: **743** 1956 Relpo A-651, 5.5" **$20-$22**
Right: **744** Napco NC8267, 5.5" **$20-$22**

Left: **745** Relpo A1136, 5.5" **$22-$25**
Right: **746** R/B Japan, 5.5" **$22-$25**

Left: **747** Lefton 032, 6.75" **$25-$28**
Center: **748** Lefton, 5.75" **$25-$28**
Right: **749** Relpo 5934, 6.5" **$25-$28**

Left: **750** A2006, 6" **$15-$18**
Center: **751** 1728, 6" **$12-$15**
Right: **752** No Mark, 6.75" **$18-$20**

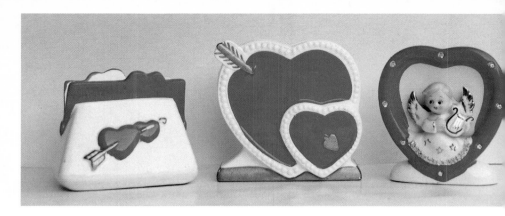

Left: **753** Rubens E9284A, 4" **$10-$12**
Center: **754** No Mark, 5.25" **$10-$12**
Right: **755** Dickson Japan, 5" **$12-$15**

Left: **756** 2772, 6.5" **$22-$25**
Right: **757** Lefton 2773, 4.25" **$22-$25**

Left: **758** Napco S692V, 4" **$15-$18**
Center: **759** R/B Japan 1459, 5.5" **$15-$18**
Right: **760** Nancy Pew Japan, 5" **$12-$15**

Left: **761** C-6636, 5.75" **$20-$22**
Center: **762** Relpo A1514, 6.25" **$25-$28**
Right: **763** Napco 3B2798, 5" **$20-$22**

764 Relpo A1019, 4" **$22-$25**

Left: **765** Napco A1746F, 3.75" **$12-$15**
Right: **766** Rubens Japan 551, 6" **$22-$25**

767 Caffco E-3290, Japan, 6.5" **$15-$18**

Left: **768** 57496, 5" **$12-$15**
Right: **769** 1963, Samson Import Co, Relpo 5390, 5" **$15-$18**

Left: **770** No Mark, 4.75" **$15-$18**
Center: **771** 1959, Samson Import Co, Relpo 355, 5" **$12-$15**
Right: **772** 1959, Rubens Originals 522, Wall Pocket, 5" **$18-$20**

Left: **773** Fine A Quality, Japan, 6" **$18-$20**
Center: **774** R/B Japan, 6.25" **$15-$18**
Right: **775** Lefton 934, Wall Pocket, 4.5" **$20-$22**

Left: **776** 1513, 4" **$10-$12**
Center: **777** Fine A Quality 57494, Japan, 4" **$10-$12**
Right: **778** R/B Japan, 4" **$12-$15**

Left: **779** Lefton 2995N, 4.5" **$12-$15**
Center: **780** CI JN-4114, 6" **$20-$22**
Right: **781** No Mark, 5" **$18-$20**

Left: **782** 1961, Samson Import Co, Relpo 5154, 4" **$12-$15**
Center: **783** No Mark, 6" **$20-$22**
Right: **784** Rubens 164, 5.25" **$18-$20**

Left: **787** No Mark, 4.75" **$10-$12**
Right: **788** Lark Japan, 5" **$10-$12**

Left: **785** Teleflora, 5" **$10-$12**
Right: **786** Napcoware C-8993, 5.25" **$15-$18**

789 Relpo C-7942, 6" **$20-$22**

Left: **790** Relpo 2073, 6.5" **$12-$15**
Right: **791** 1134, 4" **$12-$15**

Left: **792** Napco, 5.25" **$8-$10**
Center: **793** Relpo 6157, 5.5" **$8-$10**
Right: **794** No Mark, 5.25" **$8-$10**

795 Nancy Pew, 5" **$15-$18**

Left: **796** A-1986, 6" **$15-$18**
Center: **797** Napcoware C-8181, 7" **$15-$18**
Right: **798** Japan 1754, 6" **$15-$18**

799 Relpo 5796, Japan, 5" **$8-$10**